MW01074803

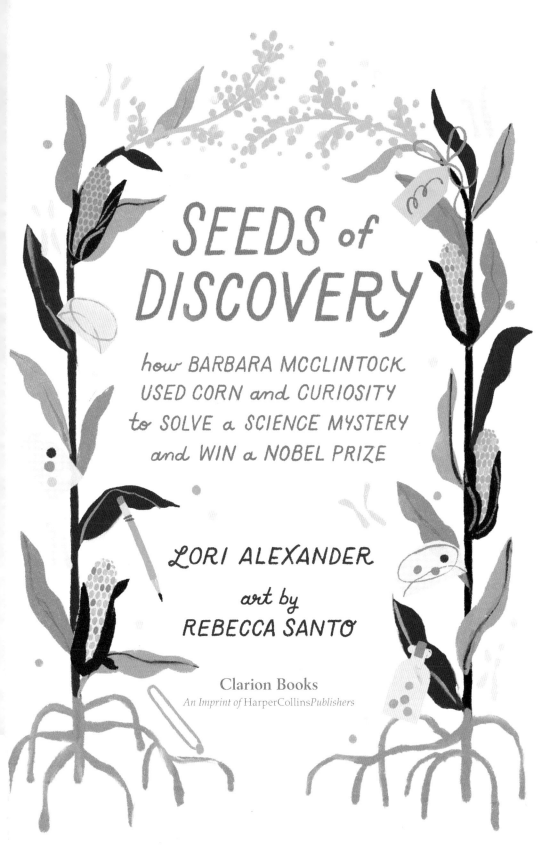

SEEDS of DISCOVERY

how BARBARA MCCLINTOCK USED CORN and CURIOSITY to SOLVE a SCIENCE MYSTERY and WIN a NOBEL PRIZE

LORI ALEXANDER

art by
REBECCA SANTO

Clarion Books
An Imprint of HarperCollins Publishers

Clarion Books is an imprint of HarperCollins Publishers

Seeds of Discovery
Text copyright © 2025 by Lori Alexander
Illustrations copyright © 2025 by Rebecca Santo
All rights reserved. Manufactured in India. No part of this book may be used
or reproduced in any manner whatsoever without written permission except in the
case of brief quotations embodied in critical articles and reviews. For information
address HarperCollins Children's Books, a division of HarperCollins Publishers,
195 Broadway, New York, NY 10007.
www.harpercollinschildrens.com
Library of Congress Control Number: 2024942228
ISBN 978-0-06-324599-0

The artist used Adobe Photoshop, Procreate, and scanned traditional textures
to create the digital illustrations for this book.
Typography by Alison Klapthor and Torborg Davern
24 25 26 27 28   REP   10 9 8 7 6 5 4 3 2 1
First Edition

For the girls who follow their passions,
no matter the obstacles
—L. A.

To Pat and Piper
—R. S.

Contents

In science, the important thing is to modify and change one's ideas as science advances.

—Claude Bernard, French scientist (1813–1878)

They thought I was crazy,
absolutely mad.

—Dr. Barbara McClintock
(1902–1992)

Introduction

Every living thing—from a pea plant to a prickly cactus, from a mouse to a moose—produces young of its own kind. These *offspring* are similar to their parents, but not exactly alike. You too share features, or *traits*, with your biological parents, things like eye color, hair color, freckles, and whether you can roll your tongue.

So how does a body have traits like curly brown hair and dimples, just because Mom or Dad has them? Why not fur or feathers or scales? The answer is in our *genes*.

Our bodies are made from trillions of tiny cells. Genes are located deep within these cells, and they give instructions to our body about how to grow and function. Genes are made from stretches of *DNA* (short for *deoxyribonucleic acid*), a chemical that holds a unique code for every living organism. Half of our DNA comes from our mother, and half comes from our father. When this DNA is shuffled together, it results in an entirely new combination—a child similar to mother, father, and siblings—but not identical to them.

Mother and father mouse produce offspring with new combinations of their traits, like fur color, fur pattern, whisker color, and ear shape.

Today, new technologies harness the power of genes and DNA to do incredible things like treat diseases, solve crimes, and create healthier foods. One day, the same technologies may re-create extinct animals, like the woolly mammoth or the dodo bird. Amazing achievements like these do not happen overnight. They are built upon years of research from many types of scientists—scientists who are inspired by big questions or small curiosities, even about something as ordinary as a kernel of corn.

This story takes place in the early 1900s, before genes and DNA were well understood, back when researchers knew far less about the way parents pass down traits to their children.

It begins with a girl who loves science.

1
Put to the Test

She grips her pencil and leans over the desk. Facts swirl in her mind. She can hardly wait to begin the test. Before the hour is up, the spaces are filled. "I knew they wouldn't ask me anything I couldn't answer." Science is her favorite subject, after all. The only thing left to do is write her name on the front page.

But . . . what *is* her name? Her mind has gone blank.

Should she ask another student? No. They might think she's "a screwball." She waits and waits, her cheeks growing hot from embarrassment. "What I was thinking about . . . was so much more important" than a name. Minutes *tick . . . tick . . . tick.* Finally, she remembers.

Her name is Barbara McClintock.

5

Her name hasn't always been Barbara. She was born Eleanor, the third daughter to a mother and father who desperately wanted a son. When her mother would become frazzled caring for three young girls all alone— her husband was busy starting a new medical practice— she'd set Eleanor on the floor with a few toys. Eleanor didn't cry out as most babies would. Every time, she happily entertained herself for hours. After four months, the family decided the name Eleanor was too sweet and delicate for such an independent child. Although the official paperwork wouldn't be filed for many more years, they began to call her by a name they believed to be stronger— Barbara. A fourth child, a son, was born about a year and a half after Barbara.

As a young girl, Barbara enjoyed chasing her brother and some other boys in their Brooklyn, New York, neighborhood.

When they played baseball, Barbara played, too. When they played football, Barbara played, too. When they climbed trees . . . *ugh*! Her foot tangled in the long fabric of her skirt. Barbara convinced her mother and the local dressmaker to add a new item to her wardrobe— bloomers—though this was a time when clothing for

girls and women was meant to be pretty, not practical. Wearing these baggy pants under a skirt was a trend many American women discouraged. However, Barbara cared more about freedom than beauty. She gathered up her skirt and climbed. "I can do anything I want," she said, catching up to the boys.

The other girls and their mothers glared and shook their heads: *Proper young ladies do not run and tumble like boys.*

Barbara was encouraged to try more acceptable sports, like ice skating and tennis. Although she enjoyed these activities, she soon found a passion for something new—learning. Barbara loved to read and spend time alone with her books, just "thinking about things."

Barbara shines in school. She especially likes math and science. When her teacher writes a problem on the board, Barbara tries to find a new way to solve it. She waves her hand, never shy about sharing her answers. But speaking up makes Barbara feel different from the other girls. They sit quietly and let the boys give all the answers. This doesn't stop Barbara. She grows accustomed to the idea that she is "a girl doing the kinds of things that girls are not supposed to do."

Barbara graduates from high school early. She wants to keep learning about science. She wants to go to college. It is 1919, and a great war has just ended in Europe. Her father has spent the last two years overseas in France working as a military doctor. Her mother gives piano lessons to earn money for food and clothes. She wants Barbara to marry and begin a family, like her older sisters have. Her mother worries that if Barbara goes to college, she will become "a strange person, a person that doesn't belong to society" and no man will ever want to marry her.

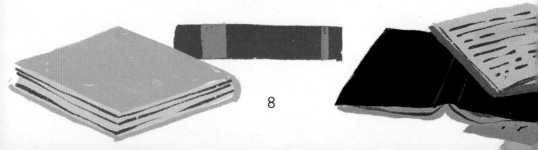

8

Barbara finds a simple office job. After work, she heads straight to the library. She reads all afternoon and into the evening. She is only sixteen years old but makes a promise to herself: she will "get the equivalent of a college education if I have to do it on my own."

Education of Girls and Women in the United States

Only one hundred years ago, schooling for girls was much different than it is today. For decades, it was assumed that girls were not interested in education

because they would never use what they learned. Most only needed housekeeping and child-rearing skills for their likely career as wife and mother. In the early 1900s, many people thought that women were not smart enough to master college-level classes. Some even believed that higher education would harm women's health, making them weak and likely to get sick. Once these ideas were disproved, more women were allowed into colleges, although these were typically schools for women only, with classes limited to home economics or training to become a teacher. By the 1960s, most colleges were open to coeducation, teaching women and men together. At that time, about 40 percent of college students were women. It wasn't until 1979 that as many women attended college as men. Today, more women than men enroll in and graduate from college.

2
Ahead of Her Time

Barbara has spent six months working and reading when her father returns home from the war. Thankfully, he supports Barbara's desire to go to college. There are several women's colleges nearby. But Barbara has her heart set on Cornell University in Ithaca, New York, a college open to both men and women.

Only a day's train ride from home, life at Cornell is more exciting than Barbara ever imaged. Over the next four years, she packs her schedule with science classes: botany (the study of plants), zoology (the study of animals), geology (the study of earth's structure), meteorology (the study of weather and climate), cytology (the study of cells), and genetics (the study of genes). She learns from professors. She learns from other students. For fun, she takes up the banjo, playing in a jazz band around town. "College was just a dream," she will say later about these happy times.

Barbara is so busy, she must cut something from her schedule. That thing is her long hair. It takes too much time to wash and style. Her new look makes "quite a noise on campus the next day." While in the coming years, short hair on women will become popular, here at Cornell, Barbara is ahead of her time.

She finishes her college education in 1923. While her mother hopes Barbara will now find the time to get married and have children, Barbara stays at Cornell to continue learning instead. As a graduate student, Barbara works with a professor who is interested in a type of corn called *maize*. This professor wants to learn more about tiny structures deep inside maize cells, called *chromosomes*. What do they look like? How many are there? He has been trying for months, but even with his microscope, he can't see chromosomes clearly.

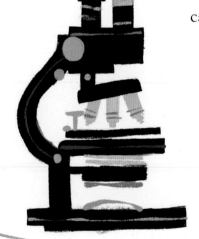

What Are Chromosomes?

The smallest living part of a plant or animal is called a cell. Simple organisms, like bacteria, are made of a single cell. To build something more complex, like a human, it takes many types of cells. These include skin cells, bone cells, muscle cells, fat cells, blood cells, and nerve cells. Inside every cell is a control center called the nucleus. And inside the nucleus, chromosomes are found. They look like thin threads and can only be seen with a microscope. Today we know chromosomes are actually small bundles of DNA. Specific sections of DNA hold codes that instruct a living thing how to grow and function. These special bits of DNA are called genes. When Barbara was in college, scientists were just beginning to learn about chromosomes. The structure of DNA and the location of genes were still a mystery.

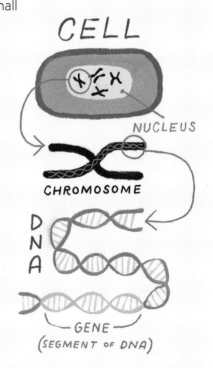

CELL

NUCLEUS

CHROMOSOME

D
N
A

— GENE —
(SEGMENT of DNA)

Barbara is eager to tackle these questions about chromosomes. First she drips red dye on the maize cells, then she adds a drop of acid to wash away some dye. This stains the chromosomes and makes them stand out. Next, she squishes the sample between two glass squares to flatten the cell nucleus. Barbara learned about this method by reading the work of John Belling, a botanist who studies chromosomes in flowering plants. She makes a few improvements to better adapt the method to her corn sample. Many discoveries in science happen this way, building upon the work of others.

Now Barbara slips the glass slide onto her microscope and peers into the eyepiece.

A bit more light.

A twist to focus.

And . . .

Look!

Barbara sees a jumble of striped chromosomes. Some bits stain darker, creating the reddish stripes or bands of color. She counts. She measures. She matches up chromosomes that have the same shape, length, and banding pattern. From Barbara's careful observation, she finds that maize cells contain twenty chromosomes, ten from each parent plant.

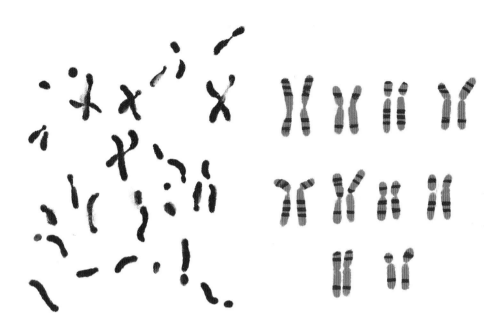

Chromosomes under a microscope, before (black) and after being stained and organized (red)

The process takes only a few days, and it's all finished: "clear, sharp, and nice." Now Barbara can easily tell one chromosome from another. She is excited by the discovery. Her professor should be excited too. Instead, he grumbles, envious of Barbara's quick success.

Who Has Chromosomes?

All living things have chromosomes in their cells. The total number of chromosomes varies by species and is not correlated to species size or complexity. Chromosomes typically come in pairs: half from the mother and half from the father.

ORGANISM	CHROMOSOMES FROM FEMALE PARENT	CHROMOSOMES FROM MALE PARENT	TOTAL CHROMOSOMES IN EACH CELL
FRUIT FLY	4	4	8
NEMATODE WORM	6	6	12
PEA PLANT	7	7	14
MAIZE PLANT	10	10	20
SNAIL	12	12	24
CAT	19	19	38
HUMAN	23	23	46
ELEPHANT	28	28	56
WOOLLY MAMMOTH	29	29	58
DOG	39	39	78
GOLDFISH	50	50	100
ADDER'S-TONGUE FERN	720	720	1440

Barbara continues to study the corn's chromosomes. She numbers the pairs one through ten, from longest to shortest. This numbering system keeps Barbara organized and will make it easier for her to compare chromosomes from one plant with those from another.

The same twenty chromosomes, with the same staining pattern, are found inside every cell of Barbara's maize plant. When she examines a second maize plant, she finds that its cells also contain a similar-looking set of twenty chromosomes, but they stain with a slightly different pattern of reddish stripes. Barbara wonders if these small differences in chromosomes have anything to do with the differences she sees in the ears of corn. She peels back a few husks and takes a peek. Some of the plants grow corn that is yellow, while other plants grow corn that is purple or red.

How do the kernels get these unique features, these *traits?*

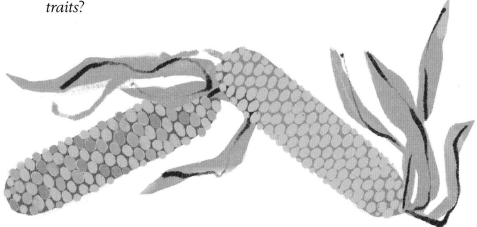

The Monk and the Pea Plants

One of the first people to closely study plant traits was Gregor Mendel. Mendel was a monk who grew a garden at his monastery in the part of Europe now known as the Czech Republic. He noticed that the pea plants had different traits: some were tall and others were short, some had purple flowers and others had white flowers, some peas were smooth while others were wrinkled. Mendel wondered why. He crossbred, or used two different varieties of plants, to grow a new plant. At that time, most people thought that traits from two plants simply blended together. So at first Mendel guessed that a tall pea plant pollinated by a short pea plant would make seeds that would grow into a medium pea plant. That's not what happened. They grew into more tall pea plants. The traits didn't mix together like paint; they stayed separate. After many years of growing and studying the plants, he discovered rules to explain why certain traits were seen more often or less often. It would take another twenty-five years—long past Mendel's death in 1884—for scientists to understand these rules about inheritance, or how traits are passed down from parents to offspring. In 1909, the word *gene* was first used to describe the unit responsible for passing along traits. But scientists still didn't know where genes were located or how they worked.

3
The Farmer Scientist

To study the traits of maize, Barbara and a few other graduate students who want to study corn need to grow more plants. This is not easy work! Out in the university fields, Barbara plants her corn in a sunny spot.

Poke a hole.

Drop a seed.

Follow the string to keep rows straight.

Poke. Drop.

Again.

Again.

Young plants must be watered daily so they don't dry out. Each one gets a tag with information about its strain, or the type of parent plants it came from.

When it's time to pollinate the plants—breed two parent plants together to make a new plant—Barbara takes

even more care. Corn plants are usually pollinated when wind carries tiny pollen grains from the tassel to the silks. But Barbara wants to crossbreed specific corn plants and not leave it up to the wind. She ties paper bags over the tassels and the ear shoots before their silks appear. Now Barbara can collect pollen from one plant and place it on the silks of another, based on the experiments she has designed. "It's such a pleasure to carry out an experiment," she says. "Carry it out and watch it go."

Barbara and the other graduate students all wake up early to begin work in the field before it gets too hot. Yet she's the only

LEAF

TASSEL

STALK

SILK

EAR

PROP ROOTS

ROOTS

one trying to farm in skirts or dresses. It's the late 1920s, still forty years before it was acceptable for the average American woman to be seen wearing pants. Barbara can no longer "live with the costumes that others had in the past." After a long day of tending the corn, she heads to the tailor and orders a pair of knickers, loose pants that extend a bit past her knees. The new garment raises eyebrows but allows for more freedom and comfort, much like the bloomers she wore as a girl.

In the fall, Barbara harvests her corn. She looks at the colors and textures of the kernels. She saves a grain of pollen from a plant's tassel, stains it with special dyes, and examines it with her microscope. She inspects the chromosomes. How do they compare to their parent plants from last season? She studies what is the same. She studies what is different. She gets better and better at telling the tiny chromosomes apart.

The type of work Barbara is conducting is called *basic research*. Basic research typically takes place in a lab setting and is fueled by curiosity. It attempts to answer the questions *what? why?* and *how?* Scientists doing basic research are free to follow any path they choose in their quest to gain information. Basic research may not result in a new invention or medicine or technology. That's the outcome of *applied research,* science that tries to solve an immediate, practical problem. Applied research is often built upon the knowledge learned from basic research.

Barbara doesn't yet know that her work on the genetics of corn will one day inspire other scientists to ask new questions and even create tools that help people with real problems, such as sickness from cancer or genetic diseases. Barbara continues her experiments for one simple reason—they fascinate her.

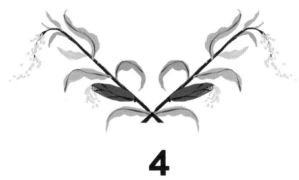

4
A Big Discovery

In 1927, Barbara earns a PhD in botany from Cornell University. She stays for several more years to continue her research. "I was just so interested in what I was doing I could hardly wait to get up in the morning and get at it," she later recalled. In addition, Cornell pays her a small sum to teach botany classes. Even though she is able to support herself, her mother still wishes she would quit science and get married. Barbara says every time she goes home for a visit, her mother tries "to persuade me to let somebody go up and get my things and not go back." But Barbara never leaves her lab for long.

Researchers want to learn how traits are passed from parents to offspring. They hope this information will one day explain how more complex issues—like diabetes, heart disease, dementia—might be passed from parents to children.

The quest to understand how traits are inherited dates back thousands of years.

Ancient farmers wondered if they could control this process while breeding two animals or two plants:

Will a large bull + a hearty dairy cow =
a larger calf that gives more meat or milk?

Will a plant with many berries + a plant
with sweet berries =
a new plant that grows many sweet berries?

Up through the early 1900s, the science behind *selective breeding*, trying to pass the most desired traits to offspring, was not fully understood. At that time, many people thought traits traveled through the blood. Expressions like "Our family bloodline" or "It's in our blood" were commonly used.

In 1930, researchers begin to think that the gene is the unit responsible for passing along traits. At this point, though, it would be impossible to develop any practical tools to control the passing-along of genes, since scientists still don't know the exact location of genes. Some scientists guess that genes are found on chromosomes, in every cell of the body, though they have no proof. Barbara wants to solve the mystery of where genes are located.

With help from a graduate student named Harriet Creighton, Barbara plans an experiment. One of her plants grows corn with waxy-feeling purple kernels. Under the microscope, its ninth chromosomes have tiny, dark-red-staining knobs on one end and skinny tips on the other end. Barbara and Harriet breed this corn with another plant that has neither waxy nor purple kernels—its ninth

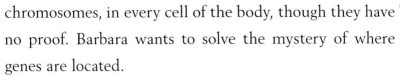

chromosomes have no knobby ends and no skinny tips.

When it comes time to harvest, they find some ears of corn are waxy and purple (like one parent) and some are neither waxy nor purple (like the other parent). But some ears are different: they are waxy *or* purple. These ears of corn inherited one trait, not both.

Under the microscope, Barbara and Harriet see the ninth chromosomes of this third type of corn has *either* the tiny knob *or* the skinny tip. Had bits of the chromosomes broken off and swapped places in the cross-pollinated plant?

Barbara and Harriet study their data and use reasoning to piece together the puzzle:

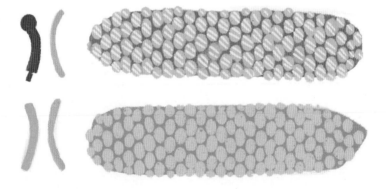

1. *If genes are responsible for passing along traits, and*

2. *If a change in the chromosomes changed the traits of the corn (texture and color),*
   then

3. *Genes must be located on chromosomes!*

Barbara and Harriet are the first to prove that genes for traits are found on chromosomes. They publish their results in a journal for other scientists to read. The discovery is huge news! Some scientists say that this work is one of the great experiments of modern biology.

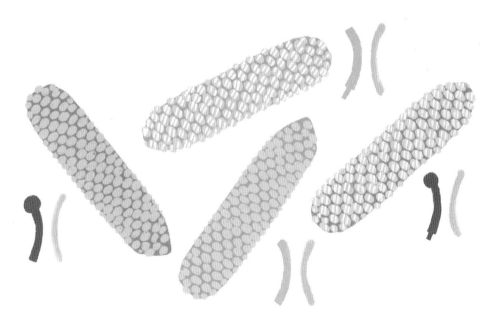

Model Organisms

Scientists often use nonhuman species—fungi, plants, or animals—in their experiments, even when they want to learn about the human body. While people look different than plants and animals, all living things share similar DNA. By studying various nonhuman species, or model organisms, and comparing their DNA to our DNA, scientists can discover much about human health and disease. Model organisms are typically easy to breed and keep in a lab. They also have a simpler structure to study. For example,

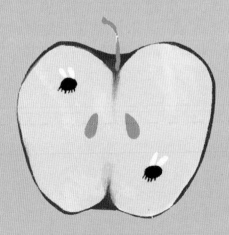

the nematode worm, used to research things like heart disease and aging, has only 959 cells (humans have more than 37 trillion). When it comes to gene research, fruit flies are among the most common models because they reproduce and grow up quickly. Two fruit flies can give birth to hundreds of offspring, which grow from eggs to adult flies in about one week. This allows scientists to study many generations in a short period of time. Corn is also useful for studying genetics. An ear of corn is actually a collection of hundreds of offspring kernels, neatly arranged onto a cob and able to be stored long term.

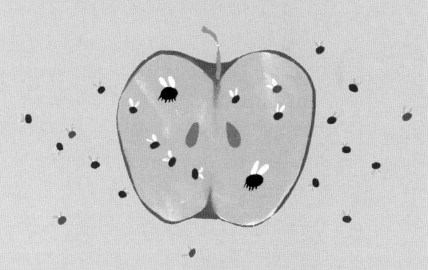

Soon Barbara's name is well-known at her university and beyond. Most scientists at this level would be given their own lab and promoted to the job of professor. Even though Cornell is open to female students, there are few openings here for female professors. It's 1932, and the United States is in the midst of the Great Depression. Jobs are hard to find for many people, especially for women in science.

Barbara could take a teaching job at an all-women's college. Or if she married a scientist, she could work in her husband's lab as his assistant. But Barbara doesn't want to be a teacher or a man's helper. She is a talented scientist in her own right.

Although she is disappointed with the university's views on hiring women, she's determined to continue her work.

It's time for Barbara to make a move.

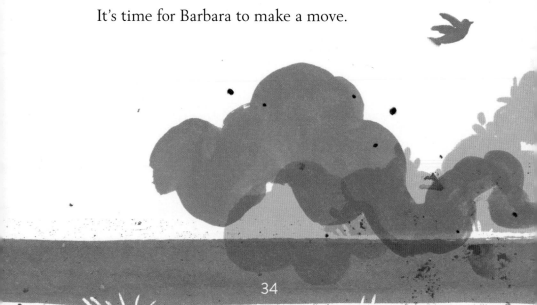

5
On the Go

Barbara packs her bags and hops into her Ford Model A. In the early 1930s, women are typically passengers, not drivers. Cars are loud, heavy, and hard to steer—many women fear breaking down or skidding off a slippery dirt road.

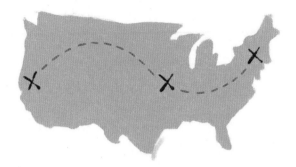

But Barbara is not afraid to take the wheel. For the next few years, she zips across the country, from New York to Missouri to California. She works in whichever labs have the space and money to fund her research. When these short-term projects end, she's off again.

In 1936, Barbara accepts a full-time position as assistant professor at the University of Missouri. She teaches classes, grades papers, and goes to meetings, all while trying to keep up with what's most important to her—her research. Barbara is still curious about traits in corn. How can she discover more about the ways that genes work?

Barbara and a coworker named Lewis Stadler begin to experiment with a new tool: the X-ray. The same technology that allows doctors to see through human tissue to view broken bones is also being used in the lab. Barbara and other scientists learn that if they expose chromosomes to X-rays, the chromosomes are left with damaged ends, much like frayed yarn in an old sweater.

Inside the X-Ray

In 1895, German physicist Wilhelm Röntgen discovered the X-ray quite by accident. He was experimenting with a type of light tube, and even though it was wrapped in heavy paper, it projected an image onto a nearby screen.

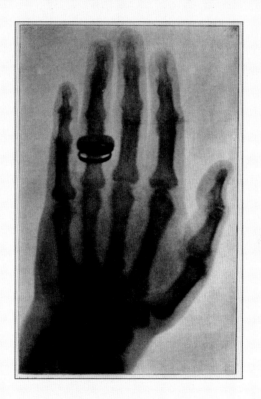

X-ray taken at Röntgen's first lecture about his new discovery, the hand of a volunteer from the audience; January 1896.

Röntgen guessed that invisible rays had passed through the paper. Since he didn't know the exact type, he called them X-rays (X standing for "unknown"). The first X-ray photo he captured was of his wife's hand. He found that the X-rays passed through skin, fat, and muscle, but dense bone—and his wife's wedding ring—blocked them, causing shadows to be cast onto the film.

Word of his discovery spread. For the first time, doctors could see inside the human body without surgery. X-ray images showed the exact location of broken bones, lodged bullets, or swallowed items. Researchers began experimenting with X-rays to determine the structure of metals, minerals, and chemical compounds in the human body. Scientists soon learned that high levels of X-ray radiation can damage living cells.

Today, X-rays are safely used for a variety of tasks like finding cavities in teeth, studying priceless artwork, and examining luggage at airports.

When Barbara plants corn whose pollen has been bombarded with X-rays, it grows ears with speckled kernels. The X-ray caused a *mutation*, a permanent change in the corn's genes, which then changed one of the corn's traits—the color of its kernels. While scientists had recently invented this method to create mutations in fruit flies, Barbara is one of the first to try it on maize. "I was very excited about what I was seeing, because many of these were new things," she will later recall. To Barbara, there's no better feeling than the thrill of discovery.

She lets her graduate students work late nights in the lab, past their eleven p.m. curfew. Still, there is more research to be done. One Sunday Barbara heads into the lab but forgets her keys. Instead of trekking all the way back home, she does the next best thing—she climbs in through the window! When other professors find out about the late nights and the unladylike climbing, Barbara gets a reputation for being a troublemaker.

Soon there are more signs that this job isn't the best fit for Barbara. The other professors stop inviting her to important meetings. Out in the cornfield, it's okay to wear knickers. But Barbara wants to wear pants *all* the time. She hasn't been promoted in five years.

We're All Mutants!

When it's time for a body to grow bigger or repair itself, it needs to create more cells. To do this, cells make a copy of their DNA and then split into two new cells. Sometimes when a cell copies its DNA, a tiny mistake happens. This switch-up in the DNA code is called a mutation. Since these copying errors occur at random, there is no predicting whether a mutation will be helpful or harmful. A helpful mutation might make an organism stronger and better able to survive in its environment. A harmful mutation might cause a disease. However, most mutations are harmless. A healthy person has more than one hundred mutations in their DNA. These little differences make us unique. Instead of waiting for mutations to happen randomly, scientists create exact mutations by using X-rays on specific chromosomes. For example, a certain mutation in fruit flies will create flies without eyes. Another will create flies that have

GENE MUTATION

NORMAL GENE

MUTATED GENE

legs growing from their heads where antennae should be. These mutations teach scientists which genes are responsible for making specific parts like eyes, legs, and antennae. Mutations cause permanent changes to genes, which may then be passed from parent to offspring. Without mutations, organisms would not change and evolve. Over millions of years, mutations create new species.

When her boss sees a wedding announcement about a *different* woman named Barbara McClintock, he calls Barbara into his office. "If you ever get married, you'll be fired," he informs her.

Like other times in her life, Barbara grows frustrated by current customs and attitudes. While stubbornness, independence, and an intense focus on work may be acceptable for a male scientist, these quirks are less tolerated in a woman.

Is there a place where Barbara can focus on her research?

Is there a place where she can be herself?

6
Putting Down Roots

There is.

Back in New York, on Long Island, there is a place just for research: Cold Spring Harbor Laboratory. Scientists and students from all over the world visit this spot. They meet and do research in the summer when they don't have classes to teach or attend. In the fall, when they return to their colleges and universities, Cold Spring Harbor grows quiet. Only a handful of scientists stay year-round.

In 1941, the director of Cold Spring Harbor invites Barbara to work and live there. He knows of her experiments and calls her "a brilliant research worker, with keen analytical powers and the perseverance to pursue a problem." Barbara settles into her new lab and begins planting her next crop of corn.

The same year, and until the end of World War II in 1945, the US federal government spends more money on basic research than any other country in the world, in the hope that the data collected will lead to new inventions and medicines that help Americans live longer lives with less disease and more comfort. Barbara's research on corn genetics fits into this national goal.

There are additional perks to working at Cold Spring Harbor. Barbara mentors students, but she has no formal classes to teach, no papers to grade. She plants her corn inside a greenhouse. She wears pants every day. "I can do what I want to do, and there are no comments. It is simply perfect." Barbara enjoys her freedom so much that working at Cold Spring Harbor "feels like no job at all." It's a bonus that she can work in the lab as late as she likes. Sometimes, she even sleeps there.

As the only corn geneticist at Cold Spring Harbor, Barbara completes every task on her own. She plants and weeds and waters. She studies roots and shoots, kernels and chromosomes. With no students or assistants to help, Barbara becomes familiar with each and every corn plant. She keeps records about their parent plants, too. She writes:

NO TWO PLANTS
ARE EXACTLY ALIKE.
THEY'RE ALL DIFFERENT,
AND AS A CONSEQUENCE,
YOU HAVE TO KNOW
THAT DIFFERENCE.
I START WITH THE
SEEDLING, AND I DON'T
WANT TO LEAVE IT.

I DON'T FEEL
I REALLY KNOW
THE STORY IF I DON'T
WATCH THE PLANT
ALL THE WAY ALONG.
SO I KNOW EVERY
PLANT IN THE
FIELD.

In 1945, Barbara finds a surprise in the greenhouse. The leaves on her new plants are splotchy. In some places, the green color is missing altogether. The corn kernels are speckled with white, too. Barbara knows that the parents of these plants didn't have leaves or kernels with missing color. She is so familiar with the parent plants, she can almost always guess what her new crop will look like. However, these plants don't have the same traits as their parents.

Why are these plants different? She did not use X-rays to create a mutation. Barbara thinks about the speckled corn day after day. Can she solve this genetic puzzle?

From her past research, Barbara knows that every cell in a corn plant should have the same set of twenty chromosomes. But when she uses her microscope to study two pollen cells from the same plant, she finds that the sets of chromosomes look slightly different. Their staining patterns are not identical, as they should be. It looks like tiny bits of chromosome nine have broken off and moved to a different spot on the chromosome.

Barbara also knows from her past experiments that genes are found on chromosomes. So when bits of chromosomes move, so do some genes. Barbara hypothesizes that these moving genes are responsible for the strange patches of missing color on her plant's leaves and kernels.

To test her theory, Barbara grows crops of corn—about 450 plants each season. Her lab bursts with tagged cobs, microscope slides, and notebooks brimming with data.

Day after day, she studies the relationship between the plants' color patterns and the striped patterns on their stained chromosomes. It takes nearly six years of planting and growing and studying for Barbara to make sense of her data.

By the late 1940s, she comes up with a new scientific model to explain the splotchy corn:

- Some genes can move from their original spot and wedge themselves into a new place on the chromosome.

- These "jumping genes" interrupt the work of their neighbor genes.

- The jumping genes act like a roadblock, preventing the color genes from doing their job.

- When color genes are blocked, corn plants grow leaves and kernels with blank patches of white.

Although it took many years of work, Barbara is overjoyed with her results. She says, "It never occurred to me that there was going to be a stumbling block. Not that I had the answer, but I had the joy of going at it. When you have that joy, you do the right experiments." As she gathers more data, she keeps an open mind about her findings: "You let the material tell you where to go . . . because you're integrating with an overall brand new pattern in mind. You're not following an old one; you are convinced of a new one."

The process that creates genetic diversity, or different traits in the same species—like breeds of dogs or varieties of apples—is still a mystery to scientists in the 1940s. Barbara has learned that when genes move to a new location on a chromosome, organisms grow to look a bit different than their parents. So her research might help to explain why there is such a variety of plants, animals, and people in the world.

Barbara is eager to learn more:

Why do genes jump?

How do genes jump?

What changes occur in an organism after genes jump?

By continuing to answer these basic research questions, she will add to the world's knowledge about genes. First, Barbara needs to spread the word about jumping genes. This will be a challenge. Her discovery goes against the current thinking about genetics. In the 1940s, most scientists believe that genes are stuck in place on chromosomes, like beads on a string. Barbara once believed in this theory as well. Based on her research, she now knows that genetic structure is much more complex, with genes moving and sections of chromosomes changing. Can she convince the other scientists?

In 1950, she writes a short paper about her discovery. It's published in a research journal. Not many scientists read it. In a time when few people own a television and the internet has not yet been invented, news travels slowly. Maybe Barbara can explain it better in person.

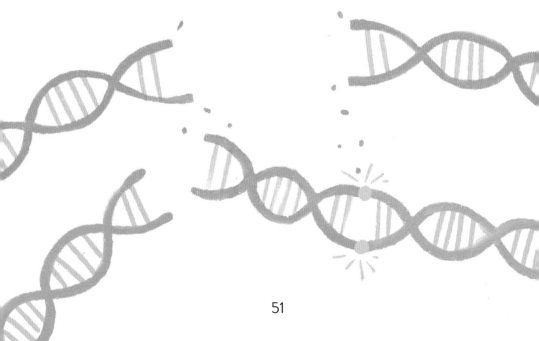

She gets her chance in the summer of 1951, when the crowds of scientists and students return to Cold Spring Harbor. There's a big conference where researchers can share their discoveries. The room is packed with three hundred scientists from all over the world. Some are famous. Some are friends, like former student Harriet Creighton.

Barbara takes the stage. Her hands sweat. Her heart sprints. She has one hour to explain the data she collected over the past six years. Will the other scientists be excited about her discovery? Will they ask good questions?

There is only one way to find out.

7

What Is She Talking About?

E ven though Barbara speaks quickly, it takes nearly two hours to deliver her presentation. When she finishes, the room is silent. No one asks a question. Some scientists shrug their shoulders. Others yawn. Finally, there is some mumbling. And then outright complaints:

Too much data!

Impossible to follow!

Downright confusing!

Her friend Harriet says the presentation "fell like a lead balloon."

Barbara's heart sinks. She is "startled they didn't understand it. Didn't take it seriously." She is a well-known scientist with many years of experience. In 1945, she had been voted president of the Genetics Society of America—the very first woman elected to this role. Why aren't they excited about her work? Was her presentation too long? Was her data too complicated?

Although Barbara has spent years completely focused on her study of jumping genes, maybe working alone was a disadvantage. As the lone corn geneticist at Cold Spring Harbor, she has had few people to share her ideas with. Few people to offer her feedback as she practiced her presentation. With additional discussion and debate, maybe Barbara would have been more skilled at communicating and explaining her research.

In 1953, Barbara tries one more time. She writes another paper. This one is longer and more complex. A few corn scientists begin to appreciate her research. Barbara wants more geneticists and biologists to see the importance of her work, though. She is certain that jumping genes exist in other organisms besides corn. Maybe jumping genes can help to explain why people become sick with diseases like cancer. Sadly, only two people request copies of her latest paper.

Some scientists agree that jumping genes exist, at least in corn. Although most are not convinced that this discovery is important. Other scientists are not open to a new way of thinking at all. Many still believe that genes are stuck on chromosomes. The beads-on-a-string theory makes sense to researchers, so they are not eager to embrace Barbara's new findings. Science often works this way. When many people think that a certain way is true or best, it tends to become a rule. That is, until one scientist sees things differently. The rule is then broken. But convincing others to change their minds is no easy task.

Barbara decides that publishing her work and giving lectures in packed auditoriums is a waste of time. Yet something inside of her does not want to quit completely:

"If you know you are on the right track, if you have this inner knowledge, then nobody can turn you off . . . no matter what they say."

For the next thirty years, Barbara studies jumping genes. She also keeps up with research happening in different areas of biology. She enjoys reading about frogs, toads, stick bugs, and the clever ways that animals mimic similar-looking animals to protect themselves from predators. She takes trips to Mexico, Colombia, and Peru with researchers who want to know where maize plants first originated. She helps other scientists with their experiments and learns from their results.

Although her big discovery about jumping genes seems to go unnoticed by fellow scientists, Barbara tries to stay positive about the break from publishing her work: "It was an opportunity I do not regret; in fact, I think it was a great opportunity not to be listened to, but to listen. Difficult as it may seem."

8
Science Marches On

While Barbara continues to study jumping genes, scientists in other parts of the world conduct their own curiosity-driven basic research. They begin looking deeper inside chromosomes and genes, all the way down to the DNA level.

In the 1950s, geneticists know that DNA is copied every time cells divide to make new cells, like when it's time for a body to grow or repair itself, although scientists don't understand how this process works. They don't know what DNA looks like. British scientist Rosalind Franklin has the idea to use X-rays to examine a crystal of DNA. When X-rays bounce off of the crystal, her assistant takes pictures. On the fifty-first attempt, they snap a photo of a hazy, striped X shape. They call it Photo 51. It doesn't look

like much, but at the time it's the best picture that's ever been taken of DNA.

A visiting scientist, James Watson, is shown Photo 51 without Rosalind's permission. He has been working with another scientist, Francis Crick, to figure out the structure of DNA. Instead of using X-rays, they use metal rods and balls to create a large model. Rosalind's photo gives Watson and Crick a clue—it reminds the scientists of a twisted ladder. They make a sketch and adjust their model. They call the twisted ladder shape a *double helix*.

Watson and Crick announce that they have just discovered "the secret of life." Soon, they publish their findings. In 1962, they receive the Nobel Prize for their discovery. Unfortunately, Rosalind died a few years earlier, so she is not officially recognized for her work.

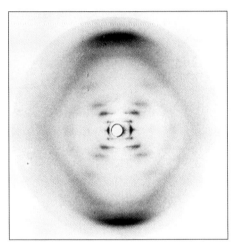 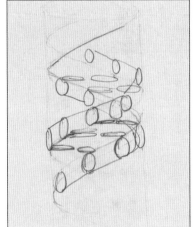

Left: Photo 51, taken by Raymond Gosling and Rosalind Franklin at King's College London, May 1952, is considered to be one of the most important pictures of all time.
Right: Sketch of DNA made by Francis Crick after seeing Photo 51. United Kingdom, 1953.

The Shape of DNA

Each "rung" of the DNA ladder is made from four different chemical compounds called bases. They are abbreviated A, T, C, and G. The bases join together in pairs—A and T fit together; C and G fit together. The order, or sequence, of these DNA base pairs is like a long code. Specific lengths of this code make up genes. The codes in your genes determine traits like your hair color, eye color, and height. At first, scientists wondered if this DNA structure was too simple—how could every living thing be created with only four different bases? Now we know that the total number of base pairs and their exact order provide enough unique combinations to account for all the variety of life on earth.

Opposite page: The structure of DNA. When it's time to for a cell to divide, the two long sides of the double helix split apart, like the two sides of a zipper. Each single strand becomes a template where a new other half is built, just like the one before.

STRUCTURE of DNA

SUGAR–
PHOSPHATE
BACKBONE

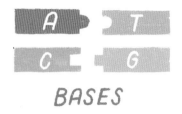

BASES

DNA CAN SPLIT...

...AND FORM
NEW STRANDS
OF DNA!

Learning the structure of DNA helps researchers who study genes and traits. Until this point, genes could only be studied by breeding plants or animals and then waiting until the next generation grew up to see what changed. Will next season's corn be a different color? Will next week's fruit flies have legs where their antennae should be? The process took time. Now scientists have a whole new way to look at genes: by studying

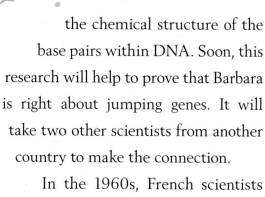

the chemical structure of the base pairs within DNA. Soon, this research will help to prove that Barbara is right about jumping genes. It will take two other scientists from another country to make the connection.

In the 1960s, French scientists Jacques Monod and François Jacob study a type of bacteria called *E. coli (short for Escherichia coli)*. They use a powerful new tool, an electron microscope, which can produce clear images of objects one thousand times smaller than the microscope Barbara uses can. With an electron microscope, Monod and Jacob discover special genes that move and regulate, or control, the work of other genes in the *E. coli* bacteria. Although they don't call their findings "jumping genes," they are very similar to what Barbara sees in her corn. The scientists publish a paper in French. The following year, they publish a longer paper in English. Barbara reads it. She is delighted!

Barbara writes a paper about the similarities between her research and the new research in bacteria. The article is published in a science journal. Shortly after, the French scientists visit Cold Spring Harbor to give a presentation. At the end of their speech, they credit Barbara as the very first person to discover moving genes that control the work of other genes. They say, "Long before regulator genes were recognized in bacteria, the extensive and penetrating work of McClintock had revealed the existence in maize." The audience chatters and buzzes, unlike the dead silence after Barbara's presentation on jumping genes. But the crowd's excitement is mostly about the new research in bacteria and less about Barbara's work.

Maybe this is because the field of *molecular biology*, studying the chemical structure of genes and DNA with high-tech methods, like electron microscopes, is popular now. In 1965 the French scientists win a Nobel Prize for their experiments with bacteria. Barbara's observations of maize chromosomes through a regular microscope seem old-fashioned to some researchers. But she believes corn has more to teach about the way genes function and move.

Slowly, other researchers begin to agree with Barbara's findings, as Monod and Jacob do. "When you know you're right, you don't care. You can't be hurt," Barbara reminds herself. "You just know . . . you may have to wait some time."

In 1967, Barbara earns a special award from the National Academy of Sciences, the most prestigious scientific society in the United States. It recognizes her as a major contributor to the field of genetics. The same year, she turns sixty-five. At that age, researchers are required to retire from Cold Spring Harbor. Barbara does not want to stop doing experiments. To reward her hard work and dedication, she's given a new title: Distinguished Service Member. She's able to keep her lab and remain in her apartment at Cold Spring Harbor.

Barbara continues to mentor young scientists and conduct research in her lab. Outside the lab, she enjoys nature walks. Even at sixty-five years old, Barbara's eyes are sharp. In spring, she spots fields of wildflowers with strange patterns of color—"It's the right pattern at the wrong place at the wrong time." She guesses that jumping genes are responsible. In fall, she gathers plump green walnuts from nearby trees. After they dry, she scoops out their insides to add to her special brownie recipe. Sometimes Barbara invites friends to her tiny one-bedroom apartment, but more often, she hosts tea and conversation in her lab, which feels more like home.

9
Catching Up

Not long after Barbara's official retirement, scientists begin to find jumping genes in other living organisms besides corn—in bacteria, viruses, fungi, yeast, fruit flies, even humans. In the mid-1970s, geneticists agree to give jumping genes a more scientific name. They call them *transposons* (trans-POH-zons), from the word *transpose*, meaning "to switch places."

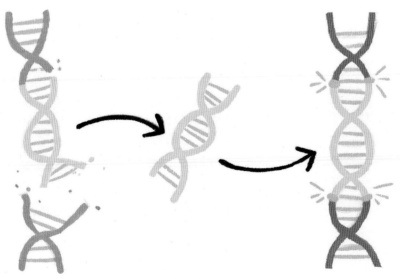

Soon, more is learned about the importance of transposons. For example, when genes jump in bacteria, the change can create *superbugs*, new strains of bacteria that are resistant to, or cannot be killed by, antibiotic medicines. Transposons may explain how normal cells turn cancerous. They also play a key role in how plants and animals evolve and adapt to a change in their environment.

"SUPERBUGS"

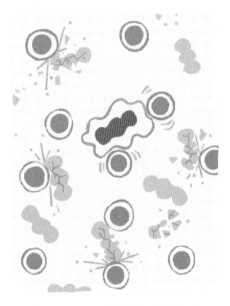

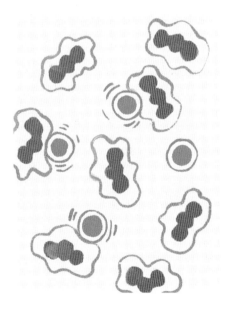

ANTIBIOTICS **KILL** NON-RESISTANT BACTERIA...

... **BUT** ANTIBIOTIC-RESISTANT BACTERIA **MULTIPLIES**

How the Peppered Moth Adapted to a Changed Environment

In the early 1800s, the peppered moth—a species of white moth with a sprinkle of black specks—could be found in many cities in England. These moths blended in perfectly with light-colored tree bark and walls, which prevented the moths from becoming a snack for hungry birds.

At this time, the Industrial Revolution was underway. Many products that were once made by hand were now made by machines. Busy factories, powered by burning coal, billowed smoke and ash into the air. The oily soot darkened tree bark and walls. Now the white moths could be easily spotted and eaten by birds. However, one moth was lucky. A transposon turned off the gene for white wings, creating wings with more black speckles. This new moth blended into the new darker surfaces. It mated and passed along the black wings to its offspring.

Over time, the generations of moths with darker coloring survived better in the polluted cities. By 1895, the peppered moth looked like a completely different, all-black species. The transposon had caused a mutation that helped the moths to better adapt to their surroundings. This process is called natural selection. In the early 1900s, when laws to control pollution were put into place, the air slowly cleared. Trees and walls grew clean and pale once again. Now the black moths stood out. They no longer survived like they once did. Natural selection began to favor the white peppered moths. By the 1960s, they were once again the most common type.

Maybe Barbara's retirement has given the other scientists a chance to catch up to her way of thinking. After building upon her work with their own experiments, they stop believing that genes are stuck in place. They agree that genes can move to new locations on chromosomes, turning nearby genes on or off, just like Barbara's research showed more than twenty years earlier.

Barbara begins to earn more recognition and awards for her work. She is the first woman to receive the National Medal of Science, the highest honor given for science in the United States. She is honored by prestigious universities like Harvard, Yale, and Cambridge.

Some of the awards come with a great deal of prize money. Barbara doesn't make a fuss. "I'm not a person who likes to accumulate things." She does buy a more reliable car and a slightly larger apartment closer to her lab.

Barbara wins eight major awards in only a few years' time. Letters flood into her office. There's always *knock-knock-knocking!* at her door. Reporters want interviews. Photographers want pictures. Students want advice. Barbara is now in her late seventies, and the attention makes her head spin. Besides, it's taking time away from what's still most important—her research.

But another surprise is around the corner. Her lab work will have to wait.

10

An Unexpected Announcement

O n the morning of October 10, 1983, Barbara begins her daily routine. A bit of breakfast. A little exercise. A few pages from a new book. Soft music wafts from her radio. Until a news person interrupts with an announcement: *The winner of the 1983 Nobel Prize in Physiology or Medicine is . . .*

BARBARA MCCLINTOCK!

"Oh dear," is the first thought that runs through her mind. Barbara likes to keep her apartment quiet, so she doesn't own a phone. There was no way for the prize committee to call her ahead of time. She hears the big news on the radio, like the rest of the world.

Barbara does not celebrate or cheer. She gets dressed in her sturdy pants and plain button-up shirt and heads out the door on a nature walk. She picks walnuts and thinks about baking a sweet treat. And for a few minutes, she thinks about how her life will change with news of the award. A Nobel Prize is not just for people in the United States. It's open to people all over the world. Winning means you are the very best in your field of study.

That afternoon, Barbara must take the stage once again. She will not give a two-hour speech about jumping genes to uninterested scientists. The news conference is packed with reporters, coworkers, and friends. And this time, everyone has questions for Barbara!

How does it feel?

Why did it take so long?

What will you do with the prize money?

Cameras flash. The audience cheers. Barbara is only the third woman to win a Nobel Prize in the category Physiology or Medicine. And she is the first scientist to win the award for studying plants. She will receive $190,000 in prize money, and because she did her research alone, she doesn't have to share the award with anyone else.

Barbara travels to Stockholm, Sweden, to officially

accept her prize. The other winners—in the categories of Chemistry, Physics, Literature, Economic Sciences, and Peace—gather at a fancy ceremony. Nearly two thousand people attend. The King of Sweden presents each winner with a certificate and a gold medal. Barbara is the only female winner in 1983.

When her name is called, Barbara crosses the stage. She has some gray hair. She has wrinkles from her time in the sun. At eighty-one years old, Barbara is small but mighty. The crowd erupts into thunderous applause. She gives a short speech in which she remarks, "It might seem unfair to reward a person for having so much pleasure over the years."

Back home, Barbara returns to her usual routine. She still puts in a full day of work at her lab. But more people call. More people stop by to ask questions. Sometimes, a line forms outside her office door. Although Barbara likes her privacy, she keeps a good sense of humor  about her fame. She even tries out a disguise to keep from being recognized.

On June 19, 1992, Barbara's close friends and coworkers host a small party for her ninetieth birthday. They present her with a special book. It's filled with letters and essays, each one a memory or a story about Barbara. Many of the letters praise Barbara for her dedication and hard work. Some state that she is an inspiration to other scientists who also find a thrill in doing basic research.

When Barbara reads the letters, her eyes glimmer. "I've had such a good time, I can't imagine having a better one. . . . I've had a very, very satisfying and interesting life."

Barbara remains true to herself. She never married or had children. She has always worn what was comfortable. She speaks her mind. She doesn't worry about impressing others. And she never gives up on her maize research. Barbara continues her experiments until the very end. Not long after her ninetieth birthday, she dies from old age.

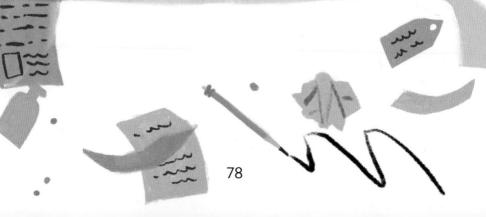

She developed a habit of calling me whenever she had something especially exciting. Not having known very much about maize genetics, it wasn't easy for me to follow. But she was very patient about describing the experiments, and she really was very confident about what she was doing. I found her absolutely fascinating.

—EVELYN WITKIN,

Geneticist at Cold Spring Harbor and friend to Barbara

To many, Barbara's methods were painfully slow: waiting for corn to sprout, comparing chromosomes from crop to crop. It took heaps of patience. She trusted herself and what she saw with her microscope. Barbara liked to offer a simple piece of advice to students beginning their own careers in science: "Take the time and look."

Recognition came slowly as well. While it took more than thirty years for Barbara to be awarded a Nobel Prize, she was able to change minds about the nature of genes. A fellow geneticist remarked, "It does not matter whether I understood Barbara completely or correctly, it only matters that in trying to understand her, my thoughts transversed new ground."

11
Building on Barbara

B arbara McClintock made key discoveries about genes, their location, and how they function. She inspired others to think differently about genes and their movement on chromosomes. Scientists continue to build on Barbara's work, as well as the work of Rosalind Franklin, James Watson, Francis Crick, and many others.

In 1990, a group of more than 2,800 researchers from six countries began working on one of the most challenging science projects of all time. They wanted to learn the exact order, or sequence, of the DNA base pairs in a set of human chromosomes. Sequencing every segment of our DNA, or *genome*, would be like having all the pages of an instruction manual on how to build a human body. Scientists called this mission the Human Genome Project.

The project would be as difficult as landing an astronaut on the moon.

Teams of biologists, engineers, computer scientists, and mathematicians used special methods and equipment to reveal the sequence of the more than three billion base pairs that make up human DNA. It took thirteen years and 2.7 billion dollars to gather and analyze this data. With team members located in the US, UK, France, Germany, Japan, and China, the project also took an incredible amount of cooperation, communication, and willingness to share data between labs. By the end of the project in 2003, scientists found that humans have about 20,500 genes in each cell.

Basic Research Creates Real-World Tools

While the Human Genome Project began as basic research to gain knowledge, it led to tools that help with practical problems. With improvements in technology, DNA sequencing now costs only a few hundred dollars and can be completed within days. Medical doctors use DNA screening tests to diagnose and treat human diseases. Forensic scientists analyze DNA sequences to solve crimes. DNA kits are also available for home use. After mailing a DNA sample (typically some cells swabbed from inside the cheek), a person can soon learn more about their traits and health—and even find distant relatives.

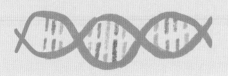

The Human Genome Project answered many questions about genes and DNA, though scientists were still curious—especially about the transposons Barbara first discovered. Once researchers finally agreed that genes could move around on chromosomes, changing the way other genes do their jobs, a world of possibilities opened up.

Instead of waiting for genes to jump at random, scientists wondered if they could control this process. In 2012, Jennifer Doudna and Emmanuelle Charpentier, created *CRISPR* (pronounced "crisper"), a system that can find specific genes inside a body, like a mutated gene that's causing a disease, then use special proteins to act like tiny scissors and cut out the harmful gene. A healthy gene can be inserted in its place. Snip and swap—like searching for a misspelled word in an essay and replacing it with the correctly spelled word. CRISPR works in every type of cell: microbes, plants, animals, and humans. This *gene editing* technology is fast and cheap, and has many promising uses. Doudna and Charpentier shared the Nobel Prize in Chemistry in 2020 for their achievement.

The CRISPR method may prove to be a cure for diseases caused by mutated genes, such as sickle cell disease, cystic fibrosis, specific types of blindness, and even some forms of cancer. Scientists are currently testing CRISPR in model organisms and in human volunteers. If practice trials show the treatment is safe and effective, it may be approved for people with these diseases.

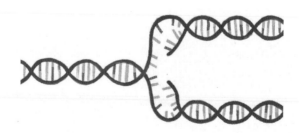

Meeting Her Hero—Almost!

Much like Barbara McClintock, Jennifer Doudna began her career in a lab doing curiosity-driven basic research. As a girl, Doudna loved reading about Rosalind Franklin and her role in discovering the structure of DNA. On a trip to Cold Spring Harbor when Doudna was twenty-three, she spotted a familiar scientist. Barbara was then in her eighties and out for one of her afternoon strolls. Doudna's heart leapt, but she was too nervous to say hello. "I felt like I was in the presence of a goddess," she later told a friend. "Here's a woman who's so famous and so incredibly influential in science acting so unassuming and walking toward her lab thinking about her next experiment. She was what I wanted to be." Barbara's work and life continue to inspire today's scientists.

In addition to the treatment of human disease, the CRISPR system is being tested in plants and animals. By removing or replacing genes, scientists can select for desired traits, like larger veggies, fruits that don't rot, or nuts without allergens. Pigs have received the CRISPR treatment as well. More than 100,000 people in the United States are waiting for lifesaving organ donations. But there aren't enough human donors to meet this need. With a bit of CRISPR gene editing, pig hearts, livers, and kidneys become compatible with human bodies.

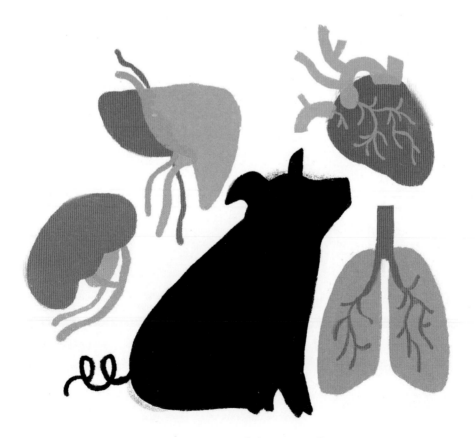

Return of the Woolly Mammoth?

Five million years ago, woolly mammoths roamed the northern parts of Asia, America, and Europe. About 10,000 years ago, the largest of these creatures died out. Scientists using CRISPR technology believe they can re-create these extinct animals. Researchers have taken DNA samples from woolly mammoths found buried in the icy permafrost in Siberia, Russia. They compared these genes to the genes of Asian elephants, the woolly mammoth's closest living relative. Scientists found about 1,600 differences, mostly in the genes that grow the shaggy hair and extra layers of fat to protect the woolly mammoth from extremely cold temperatures. By using CRISPR, scientists could edit these 1,600 genes in the cell of an Asian elephant. This cell could be turned into an embryo and placed inside of an Asian elephant or an artificial womb. About two years later, a baby elephant-mammoth hybrid would be born.

Why would anyone want to do such a thing? There is some evidence that the return of woolly mammoths could help with climate change. Currently, thick layers of snow are acting like a warm blanket over the ground in the arctic tundra. The winter cold can't penetrate deeply into the soil to keep it frozen. If this permafrost layer melts, it will release tons of planet-warming gases created by dead plants trapped inside the icy ground for more than 500,000 years. But if woolly mammoths are reintroduced to this area, perhaps they could trample and scrape away the thick snowy cover, allowing the ground to stay frozen for longer.

The Human Genome Project and CRISPR technology are two exciting advances in the field of genetics. This area of science continues to grow and evolve as researchers learn new ways to harness the power of genes and DNA.

Tinkering with Nature

If gene-editing tools like CRISPR can cure disease in an adult, why not fix problems sooner? It's possible to test a human *embryo*, an early stage of growth, and repair harmful mutations before a baby is even born. Most people agree that curing disease is a good use of CRISPR. But if it becomes acceptable

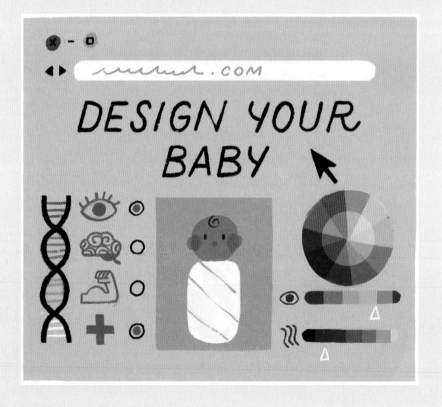

to change an unborn baby's DNA, what's stopping us from tinkering around with other genes? Would it be possible to request a baby with green eyes and brown hair? What about adding genes for height, larger muscles, stronger bones, and higher intelligence? This may seem harmless, but when these "designer babies" grow up, the traits will be passed along to their children. Over many generations, modified humans could alter the genome of our entire species.

Some scientists fear that gene editing tools could be used for darker purposes, like the production of biological weapons—living organisms designed to attack other living things. What would happen if CRISPR is used to alter bacteria or viruses into more contagious or deadly versions?

While CRISPR has many possibilities, the method also raises questions. Namely, who will police a technology that has the power to control the evolution of every species on the planet? Scientists from all over the world meet yearly to discuss the best ways to manage this powerful tool.

12
Alone in Her Field

Barbara's curiosity and problem-solving skills helped to make her a successful scientist. Perhaps even more important was her dedication to and confidence in her own ideas. It surely took courage to stay the course. Often, her work went unnoticed by her peers. At other times, she was judged harshly—whispers that she was "more boy than girl" because of her short hair and practical clothing—simply for being herself.

Maybe feeling like an outsider motivated Barbara to focus on her work all the more. Her corn research spanned decades, and her findings on transposons were eventually called "one of the two great discoveries of our times in genetics" by the Nobel Prize Committee (the other being the structure of DNA).

One thing is certain—Barbara was fascinated by the questions she asked and the answers she uncovered. Thinking back on her long career, Barbara remarked, "I just have been so interested in what I was doing, and it's been such a pleasure, such a deep pleasure, that I never thought of stopping."

Much like relay racers handing off a baton, today's basic researchers rely on the next generation to continue their work and apply it to everyday problems. These future scientists will need curiosity, dedication, and fresh ideas—the same talents Barbara possessed—to keep science moving forward. Whether in genetics, or another branch of science like chemistry or physics, or a different field altogether, new discoveries are built upon old discoveries, advancing our knowledge and improving our lives.

Maybe one of these future scientists will be you.

Time Line of Events

June 16, 1902

Eleanor McClintock, later renamed Barbara, is born in Hartford, Connecticut, to Sara Handy and Thomas Henry McClintock.

1908

The McClintock family moves to Brooklyn, New York.

1914

World War I begins.

1917

The US enters the war and Thomas McClintock is sent overseas as a military surgeon.

1918

World War I ends, and Barbara's father returns home.

1919

Barbara is accepted into Cornell University in Ithaca, New York.

1923

Barbara graduates from Cornell with a bachelor's degree in botany.

1927

Barbara earns her PhD in botany from Cornell.

1929–about 1939

An economic crisis, later named the Great Depression, causes many people to lose their jobs and homes, and they have difficulty paying for food.

March 1931

German scientists Max Knoll and Ernst Ruska give the first demonstration of their invention, the electron microscope.

August 1931

Harriet Creighton and Barbara McClintock publish a groundbreaking paper on the genetics of maize in the *Proceedings of the National Academy of Sciences.*

1936

Barbara accepts a position as assistant professor at the University of Missouri.

1939

Barbara is elected vice president of the Genetics Society of America.

September 1, 1939

World War II begins in Europe.

1941

Barbara begins working at Cold Spring Harbor laboratories in Long Island, New York. She remains there for the rest of her career.

1945

Barbara is the first woman elected as president of the Genetics Society of America.

September 2, 1945

World War II ends.

1950

Barbara publishes her first paper about jumping genes.

1951

Barbara presents her research in front of an audience at Cold Spring Harbor.

1952

Photo 51 is taken by Rosalind Franklin and Raymond Gosling. It reveals new information about the structure of DNA.

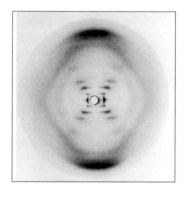

April 1953

James Watson and Frances Crick announce the structure of DNA.

November 1953

Barbara publishes a second, longer paper on jumping genes.

1960

French scientists François Jacob and Jacques Monod discover genes that move and control other genes in the bacteria *E. coli*.

1967

At age sixty-five, Barbara retires from her position at Cold Spring Harbor but keeps her lab and continues to mentor young scientists and do new research.

1971

Barbara is the first woman to be honored with the National Medal of Science.

1983

Barbara receives the Nobel Prize in Physiology or Medicine.

June 16, 1992

Barbara turns ninety. Her
friends and coworkers host
a party and present her with
a memory book filled with
the ways she influenced their
scientific careers.

September 2, 1992

After a brief illness, Barbara
dies in Huntington, New York.

2003

After thirteen years, 2,800
scientists from six countries
complete the Human Genome
Project. The project reveals
the "code" for human life—
the exact sequence of three
billion base pairs of DNA and
20,500 genes—which can now
be used by researchers and
doctors to treat, prevent, and
cure disease.

2012

CRISPR-Cas9 is invented by Jennifer Doudna and Emmanuelle Charpentier. The method allows scientists to target specific sections of genetic code, providing a precise, quick, and inexpensive way to edit genes.

2020

A CRISPR gene-editing experiment allows patients with vision loss to see color again.

2020

Jennifer Doudna and Emmanuelle Charpentier share the Nobel Prize in Chemistry for their discovery of CRISPR-Cas9 gene editing.

2023

The US Food and Drug Administration approves the first CRISPR treatment for sickle cell disease.

Glossary

bacteria—tiny living organisms, usually made of a single cell; while most bacteria are helpful, some may cause disease in humans, animals, and plants

cells—tiny structures that make up all living things

chromosomes—thin, threadlike strands of DNA coiled inside in a cell's nucleus

CRISPR—a new technology that enables researchers to edit parts of the genome by removing, adding, or altering precise sections of the DNA sequence; this method may help to cure genetic diseases

cystic fibrosis—a genetic disease that causes cells in the lungs to create sticky mucus that blocks airways, making it difficult for a person to breathe

DNA—short for *deoxyribonucleic acid*; the chemical substance in cells that stores the instructions for growth and development of living things; made of four bases: A (adenine), T (thymine), C (cytosine), and G (guanine)

DNA sequence—the exact order of base pairs in DNA, telling scientists which stretches of DNA carry genes and which do not

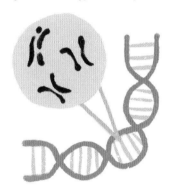

double helix—the twisted ladder shape of DNA

evolution—the gradual process by which living organisms change over time, generation after generation, through the process of natural selection

gene—a specific length of DNA that determines an organism's traits; genes are located on chromosomes

gene editing—changing an organism's DNA by adding, removing, or replacing genes

genetics—the study of genes and how traits are passed from parents to offspring

genome—the complete set of genes located on all chromosomes of a living thing

inheritance—traits passed down from parent to offspring

jumping gene—a bit of DNA that moves to a new spot on a chromosome or to a different chromosome, affecting the work of nearby genes; also called a **transposon**

maize—a type of corn plant useful as a model to study genetics

microscope—an instrument for viewing items too small to see clearly with human eyes; a *light microscope* uses visible light and lenses to magnify an object up to one thousand times its actual size; an *electron microscope* uses beams of electrons to magnify an object up to one million times its actual size

molecular biology—the study of molecules, the smallest particles of a substance, and how they interact with one another in living organisms to perform the functions of life

mutation—a random change in a gene or genes that may be passed down to offspring

natural selection—the process by which living things have traits that allow them to better adapt to their environment, making them more likely to survive and produce offspring; the main mechanism of **evolution**

nucleus—the part of a cell that stores chromosomes

offspring—the young of an organism; a parent's child or children

organism—a living thing such as an animal, plant, or single-celled life-form

pollination—when "male" pollen grains land on "female" parts of a plant to begin the process of plant reproduction

selective breeding—choosing parents with specific features to breed together to produce offspring with more desirable traits

sickle cell disease—a genetic disease that causes red blood cells to be shaped like crescents instead of concave discs; these misshapen cells block blood flow to organs and cause blood to be low in oxygen, which may result in fatigue, pain, or even death in patients with this condition

species—a group of living organisms that are genetically similar and can mate with each other

trait—a physical or behavioral characteristic controlled by genes

transposon—a bit of DNA that moves to a new spot on a chromosome or to a different chromosome affecting the work of nearby genes; nicknamed **jumping gene**

Source Notes

1. Put to the Test

"I knew they wouldn't ask me": Keller, *A Feeling for the Organism*, p. 36.

"a screwball": Ibid.

"so much more important": Ibid.

"I can do anything I want": Ibid., p. 24.

"thinking about things": Ibid., p. 22.

"a girl doing the kinds of things": Ibid., p. 27.

"a strange person": Ibid.

"get the equivalent of a college education": Ibid., p. 30.

2. Ahead of Her Time

"College was just a dream": Keller, *A Feeling for the Organism*, p. 31.

"quite a noise on campus": Ibid., p. 33.

"clear, sharp, and nice": Ibid., p. 40.

"we could tell one chromosome from another": Ibid.

3. The Farmer Scientist

"It's such a pleasure to carry out": McGrayne, *Nobel Prize Women in Science*, p. 173.

"live with the costumes": Keller, *A Feeling for the Organism*, p. 34.

4. A Big Discovery

"I was just so interested": Keller, *A Feeling for the Organism*, p. 70.

"try to persuade me": McGrayne, *Nobel Prize Women in Science*, p. 154.

"one of the truly great experiments": Gabriel and Fogel, *Great Experiments in Biology*, p. 268.

5. On the Go

"I was very excited about what I was seeing": Keller, *A Feeling for the Organism*, p. 65.

"I don't see how people can do all three": McClintock, letter to Charles Burnham, p. 1.

"If you ever get married": McGrayne, *Nobel Prize Women in Science*, p. 144.

6. Putting Down Roots

"a brilliant research worker": Fine, *Barbara McClintock*, p. 56.

"I can do what I want to do": McGrayne, *Nobel Prize Women in Science*, p. 163.

"feels like no job at all": Ibid.

"No two plants are exactly alike": Keller, *A Feeling for the Organism*, p. 198.

"went straight on it and worked quite hard": McGrayne, *Nobel Prize Women in Science*, p. 166.

"It never occurred to me": Keller, *A Feeling for the Organism*, p. 125.

"You let the material tell you": Ibid.

7. What Is She Talking About?

"fell like a lead balloon": McGrayne, *Nobel Prize Women in Science*, p. 168.

"startled they didn't understand it": Ibid., 169.

"If you know you are on the right track": McClintock, www.nobelprize.org.

"[I]t was an opportunity": Keller, *A Feeling for the Organism*, p. 143.

8. Science Marches On

"the secret of life": Markel, www.washingtonpost.com
/outlook/2021/09/13/ugly-truth-behind-discovery-dna/

"Long before regulator genes were recognized": Comfort,
The Tangled Field, p. 208.

"When you know you're right": McGrayne, *Nobel Prize
Women in Science*, p. 173.

"It's the right pattern at the wrong place": Ibid., p. 169.

9. Catching Up

"I'm not a person who likes to accumulate things":
McGrayne, *Nobel Prize Women in Science*, p. 172.

10. An Unexpected Announcement

"It might seem unfair to reward a person": McGrayne,
Nobel Prize Women in Science, p. 173.

"She developed a habit": Witkin, *On Barbara
McClintock*.

"I've had such a good time": McGrayne, *Nobel Prize
Women in Science*, p. 173.

"[T]ake the time and look": Keller, *A Feeling for the
Organism*, p. 206.

"It does not matter whether I understood": Comfort, *The
Tangled Field*, p. 267.

11. Building on Barbara

"I felt like I was in the presence of a goddess": Isaacson,
     The Code Breaker, p. 33.

12. Alone in Her Field

"more boy than girl": McGrayne, *Nobel Prize Women in
     Science*, p. 159.

"one of the two great discoveries": Ibid., p. 172.

"I just have been so interested": Ibid., p. 173.

Selected Bibliography

Chomet, Paul, and Rob Martienssen. "Barbara McClintock's Final Years as Nobelist and Mentor: A Memoir." *Cell*, vol. 170, no. 6, Sept. 2017, pp. 1049–1054.

Cold Spring Harbor Laboratory. Archive holdings, "Barbara McClintock." Accessed September 2021. www.cshl.edu/personal-collections /barbara-mcclintock/.

———."Oral History Collection: Barbara McClintock." Accessed September 2021. http://library.cshl.edu /oralhistory/topic/cshl/barbara-mcclintock/.

Comfort, Nathaniel C. *The Tangled Field: Barbara McClintock's Search for the Patterns of Genetic Control.* Harvard University Press, 2001.

Creighton, Harriet B., and Barbara McClintock. "A Correlation of Cytological and Genetical Crossing-over in Zea Mays." *Proceedings of the National Academy of Sciences*, vol. 17, no. 8, Aug. 1931, pp. 492–497.

Devereux, Paul J., and Judith Delaney. "Understanding Gender Differences in STEM." *VOX, CEPR Policy Portal*, 2019. https://voxeu.org/article /understanding-gender-differences-stem.

Doudna, Jennifer A., and Samuel H. Sternberg. *A Crack in Creation: Gene Editing and the Unthinkable Power to Control Evolution*. Mariner Books/Houghton Mifflin Harcourt, 2018.

Eisenmann, Linda. "The Impact of Historical Expectations on Women's Higher Education." Forum on Public Policy, 2006. Accessed September 2021. https://files.eric.ed.gov/fulltext/EJ1099152.pdf.

Gabriel, Mordecai L., and Seymour Fogel, eds. *Great Experiments in Biology*. Prentice-Hall, 1955. October 2021. https://archive.org/details /greatexperiments0000unse_u8y5.

Kass, Lee B. "Records and Recollections: A New Look at Barbara McClintock, Nobel-Prize-Winning Geneticist." *Genetics*, vol. 164, no. 4, Aug. 2003, pp. 1251–1260.

Keller, Evelyn Fox. *A Feeling for the Organism: The Life and Work of Barbara McClintock*. Henry Holt, 2003.

Kolata, Gina. "Dr. Barbara McClintock, 90, Gene Research Pioneer, Dies." *The New York Times*, Sept. 4, 1992. Accessed March 2022. www.nytimes .com/1992/09/04/us/dr-barbara-mcclintock-90 -gene-research-pioneer-dies.html.

McClintock, Barbara. "Induction of Instability at Selected Loci in Maize." *Genetics*, vol. 38, no. 6, Nov. 1953, pp. 579–599.

———. Letter to Charles Burnham, Oct. 9, 1940. National Library of Medicine Profiles in Science. "The Barbara McClintock Papers." Accessed September 2021. https://profiles.nlm.nih.gov/spotlight/ll /browse/all-documents.

McGrayne, Sharon Bertsch. *Nobel Prize Women in Science: Their Lives, Struggles, and Momentous Discoveries*, 2nd ed., Joseph Henry Press, 2006.

National Institutes of Health. "Human Genome Project." Accessed November 2021. www.genome.gov /human-genome-project.

NobelPrize.org. "Women Who Changed Science: Barbara McClintock." Accessed October 2021. www .nobelprize.org/womenwhochangedscience/stories /barbara-mcclintock.

van't Hof, Arjen E., Pascal Campagne, Daniel J. Rigden et al. "The Industrial Melanism Mutation in British Peppered Moths Is a Transposable Element." *Nature*, vol. 534, June 2016, pp. 102–105.

Wetzel, Corryn. "These Scientists Plan to Fully Resurrect a Woolly Mammoth Within the Decade." *Smithsonian Magazine*. September 14, 2021. www .smithsonianmag.com/smart-news/these-scientists -plan-to-fully-resurrect-a-woolly-mammoth-within -the-decade-180978655/.

Wilford, John Noble. "A Brilliant Loner in Love with Genetics." *The New York Times*, Oct. 11, 1983. Accessed November 2021. www.nytimes .com/1983/10/11/science/woman-in-the-news -a-brilliant-loner-in-love-with-genetics.html.

Witkin, Evelyn. "On Barbara McClintock: Personal Friend." Cold Spring Harbor Oral History Collection. Accessed March 2022. http://library.cshl.edu /oralhistory/interview/cshl/barbara-mcclintock /witkin-barbara-mcclintock-personal-friend/.

For Young Readers

Davies, Nicola, and Emily Sutton. *Grow: Secrets of Our DNA*. Candlewick Press, 2020.

Fine, Edith Hope. *Barbara McClintock: Nobel Prize Geneticist*. Enslow Publishers, Inc., 1998.

Isaacson, Walter. *The Code Breaker: Jennifer Doudna and the Race to Understand Our Genetic Code*. Young Readers Edition. Simon & Schuster Books for Young Readers, 2021.

Pasachoff, Naomi E. *Barbara McClintock: Genius of Genetics*. Enslow Publishers, 2006.

Ridge, Yolanda, and Alex Boersma. *CRISPR: A Powerful Way to Change DNA*. Annick Press Ltd., 2020.

Swaby, Rachel. *Trailblazers: 33 Women in Science Who Changed the World*. Delacorte Press, 2016.

Thomas, Isabel, and Daniel Egnéus. *Moth: An Evolution Story*. Bloomsbury Children's Books, 2019.

Woollard, Alison, and Sophie Gilbert. *The DNA Book: Discover What Makes You You*. DK Publishing, 2020.

Photo Credits

page 37:
Everett Collection Historical / Alamy Stock Photo

page 61 (left):
King's College London: College Archives, KING'S COLLEGE LONDON: Department of Biophysics records KDBP/1/1, Glass and acetate slides (1949-1984)

page 61 (right):
Crick, Francis, Creator. Sketch of the DNA Double Helix by Francis Crick. [Place of Publication Not Identified: Publisher Not Identified] Photograph. Retrieved from the Library of Congress, www.loc.gov /item/2021669916/.

page 77:
Barbara McClintock Papers, American Philosophical Society

Index

Note: Page references in italics indicate photographs and images

basic research of, 46
definition of, 12, 104
McClintock study of, 66, 78, 96
previous theory of, 51
study of corn chromosomes, 26, 33
traits and inheritance, 20, 27–28
Genetics Society of America, 54, 97
genome, 80, 91, 104
   See also Human Genome Project
Gosling, Raymond, 61, 98

H

Human Genome Project, 80–83, 89, 100

J

Jacob, François, 64–66, 99
jumping gene theory
   debate over, 56
   definition of, 104
   McClintock conference presentation on, 53–55
   McClintock paper on, 56, 98
   McClintock's Nobel Prize for, 75
   McClintock's study of, 57, 59
   McClintock's theory of, 49–50
   in other living organisms, 68
   previous theory of, 51
   proof of theory, 64–66

K

Knoll, Max, 96

M

maize
   growing and pollinating corn, 22, 24–25
   study of chromosomes, 16, 19, 26
   X-rays and, 39
McClintock, Barbara (Eleanor)
   career of, 34–36, 39, 42, 44, 66, 77–78, 92–93, 97, 100
   childhood of, 5–8, 95
   clothing of, 6, 25
   at Cornell University, 12–14, 27, 95–96
   credit for her work, 65–66, 72–74
   National Academy of Sciences special award, 66, 99
   Nobel Prize in Physiology or Medicine, 74–77, 92, 99
   study of corn chromosomes, 16–17, 19, 29–30, 39, 46–48, 96, 98
   See also Cold Spring Harbor Laboratory; jumping gene theory
McClintock, Sara Handy and Thomas Henry, 95
Mendel, Gregor, 20
microscope, 14–16, 25, 29–30, 48
   See also electron microscope
model organisms, 32–33, 84
molecular biology, 65, 105

119